siamese

persian

devon rex

turkish angora

himalayan

american shorthair

japanese bob

sphynx

scottish fold

american curl

ragdoll

man

siamese   persian   devon rex   turkish angora

malayan   american shorthair   japanese bob   sphynx

x   american curl   ragdoll   manx

Cat Poems

by Dave Crawley

Mee-\-Yowl!

Illustrations by Tamara Petrosino

Wordsong
Boyds Mills Press

To Lucky Tiger, the little stray who stayed—and Laurel,
who convinced him
                        —D. C.

To Charlie, Daisy, Sandy, Mickey, Vinnie, Sterling,
and all my animal inspirations, with love
                        —T. P.

Text copyright © 2005 by Dave Crawley
Illustrations copyright © 2005 by Tamara Petrosino
All rights reserved

Published by Boyds Mills Press, Inc.
A Highlights Company
815 Church Street
Honesdale, Pennsylvania 18431
Printed in China

   Library of Congress Cataloging-in-Publication Data

Crawley, Dave.
  Cat poems / by Dave Crawley ; with illustrations by Tamara Petrosino.
     p. cm.
   ISBN 1-59078-287-9 (alk. paper)
  1. Cats—Juvenile poetry. 2. Children's poetry, American. I. Petrosino,Tamara. II. Title.

  PS3603.R399C38 2005
  811'.6--dc22

2004020095

First edition, 2005
The text is set in 14-point Times Roman.
The illustrations are done in pen and ink and watercolor.

Visit our Web site at www.boydsmillspress.com

10 9 8 7 6 5 4 3 2

Contents

BRAND X

Photographers took photographs
and busy writers wrote
as groomers groomed and strokers stroked
and combers combed his coat.

Though Malabar was nonchalant,
his owner watched with pride.
This cat was chosen in a search
conducted nationwide!

His time had come to be a star.
His mission was to eat
a feast prepared by Fluffyfood,
the famous kitty treat.

They also scooped another brand—
he simply had to choose
as cameras rolled and watchers clapped.
There's no way he could lose.

But when at last they shot the ad
one thing they hadn't planned:
Malabar the TV star
preferred the other brand!

SLEEPER

She slouched on the couch.

She sprawled in the hall.

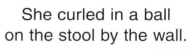

She curled in a ball
on the stool by the wall.

She snoozed on the shoes
tucked under the bed,

on the ironing board,

and the sled in the shed.

On the brink of the sink.

On the edge of a ledge.

She yawned on the lawn
and crawled under the hedge.

The very top stair,

the living room chair.

She doesn't care,
she'll sleep anywhere.

STAY, LITTLE STRAY

Stay, little stray, don't go away.
You look so hungry and thin.
Don't be so shy; there's no need to cry.
Don't be afraid to come in.

Here is a dish; eat as you wish.
No need to forage and roam.
I'm stroking your fur, hearing you purr.
Tiger, you just found a home!

7

MIND READER

My cat can't read, can't read a word.
(To think he could would be absurd.)
Yet every time I read a book,
he scrambles up to take a look.
He stops and flops on chapter one.
I'll never get my homework done!
I tip my book; he thinks it's play.
He won't get up and go away.
So in the end, I let him win.
I close my book and scratch his chin.

I think I see a little smirk.
He knew I didn't want to work.
My cat can't read, although I find
he *does* know how to read my mind!

FINICKY FELICIA

Felicia the finicky cat
will not chase a mouse or a rat.
She finds it absurd
to go after a bird.
Put food in a bowl, and that's that!

GROCERY STORE CAT

He sits by himself
on the window shelf
in old Mister Galligan's store.
If you're passing by
and he catches your eye,
you can't help but walk through the door.

He purrs right on cue
as customers coo
and more and more visitors stop.
And once they're inside
they often decide:
"We may as well stay here and shop."

They pick up potatoes,
baked beans, and tomatoes,
while now and then pausing to chat.
As they walk down the aisles,
Mister Galligan smiles—
and winks at the grocery store cat.

CAT TALK

Most cats simply say
"Meow!"
But when she's on the prowl,
Allison the alley cat
lets out a loud
"Mee-YOWL!"

Mee-Y-YOWL!

ALLEY CAT GREETING

He flattens his ears, arches his back
and gives a hiss of warning.
He won't attack, it's just his knack
for wishing me "Good morning!"

MY CAT WON'T FETCH

My cat won't fetch
a ball or stick.
He hasn't learned
a single trick.

If I command
that he should "Stay!"
he gives a yawn
and walks away.

When I say "Sit!"
he rolls around.
When I say "Come!"
he can't be found.

He knows I'll feed
him anyway,
and play the games
he wants to play.

I guess it's not
too hard to tell:
my cat has trained
me very well!

13

SEVENTEEN CATS

Cat-loving Kevin
has seventeen cats.
They flop on his counter.
They hide in his hats.

Seventeen dinners
are set in a line,
seventeen saucers
and balls of red twine.

Seventeen cats
in bed every night.
They nuzzle his nose
and snuggle up tight.

The house becomes quiet,
and nobody stirs—
except for the rumble
of seventeen purrs.

PLAYGROUND CAT

The children leave
their slides and swings
to watch him play
with shoelace strings.

He swats! He leaps!
The playground cat
does tumbles like
an acrobat.

No seesaws, slides,
or swings for him.
He doesn't need
a jungle gym.

One string—that's all.
He'll stay all day.
The playground cat
just wants to play.

TRAPPED!

I can't get up!
There's a cat on my lap!
What a terrible time
he picked for a nap.

I can't get up!
No dinner for me.
I can't play games
or watch TV.

I can't get up!
No school in the morning!
My cat dozed off
without any warning.

I can't get up!
And I don't dare speak!
I may be here
the rest of the week.

CATNAP

Eyes blinking sleepily, just before dawn,
he stirs at the foot of my bed,
greeting the day with a satisfied yawn
while stretching and bowing his head.

Now he approaches and gives me a nudge,
awaiting the touch of my hand.
Snuggling closer, he knows I won't budge.
His wish is my drowsy command.

Not ready yet for the morning alarm,
with dreamland appointments to keep,
he cuddles up close in the crook of my arm.
Together, we drift back to sleep.

ZIP-ZOOM!

Zip-zong-zoom!
Across the room!
Zap-zang-zing!
Watch him spring!
Zig-zag-zop!
The cat can't stop!

Hurry-scurry!
Flutter-flurry!
Running! Racing!
What's he chasing?
Could it be
that we can't see
what makes him dash
and clatter-crash?

20

Swirling-whirling!
Spin-and-twirling!
Round and round!
He's
    slowing
        down.

Speed diminished.
Now . . . he's . . . finished.
Flup . . . Flop . . . flap.

It's time
    to
        nap.

21

PICKING FRIENDS

He always goes
to those
who don't much care
for cats,
and with puzzling persistence
rubs the cuffs
of guests
who look away,
ignoring his existence.

And yet
he turns his back
on friends of cats,
who cluck and coo
and call his name
in vain.
From those who love him most
he keeps his distance.

EVERYONE WAS ASLEEP

Everyone was asleep but the cat
when Sammy decided to fly like a bat.
Down in the kitchen the racket began,
with clattering cups and the crash of a pan.

My parents woke up.
My sister woke, too,
disturbed by the midnight hullabaloo.
Next thing I knew he was under my sheet,
nipping my ankles and licking my feet!

"Get off me!" I hollered. He leaped to the floor,
scattering toys as he dashed through the door.
Exhausted at last, he collapsed in a heap.
It took me forever to get back to sleep.

The following morning I woke with a groan.
My parents were yawning (I wasn't alone).
And Sammy was snoozing. Can you believe that?
Everyone was awake—
but the cat.

INSIDE OUT

You want to come in,
you want to go out.
You claw at the screen,
you're pacing about.

"Meow! Let me out!"
I open the door.
I know you'll be back
in two minutes more.

The weather's too cold.
The house is too hot.
You always demand
to be somewhere you're not.

If you don't decide,
without any doubt—
you'll end up turning
us *both* inside out!

CAT BATH

Don't ever try to wash a cat.
It simply doesn't work.
If you should put her in the tub,
the cat will go berserk.

She'll growl and yowl and splash about.
She'll soak you to the skin.
And when at last you dry her off,
she'll promptly lick her chin.

She'll lick her paws, her front and back.
She makes it very plain
that all the effort you put in
has just gone down the drain.

AWFUL DAY

I had an awful day at school.
My teacher made a fuss.
I didn't get my homework in,
and then I missed the bus.

A barking dog just chased me home.
Oh no! I've lost my key!
I'll crawl in through the window. Ouch!
I think I scraped my knee!

The television doesn't work.
I can't take any more!
But now I see that Melanie
is strolling through the door.

She rubs her head against my leg,
and I'm no longer sad—
for suddenly my awful day
is really not so bad.

26

MIXED-UP MAX

My Max is a mix of this and that
(a sort of combination cat).
Part calico, part Siamese,
and orange tabby, if you please.

But Percy has a perfect pet,
a fact he won't let me forget.
"My Persian cat," he says with glee,
"is just as pure as pure can be."

I must admit, her silky coat
would make an owner want to gloat.
My mongrel Max is just a "mutt."
But now he has a cause to strut.

Though Percy's cat is meant to breed,
her litter left him shocked indeed!
There's just no way to hide the facts:

her kittens look a lot like
Max!

CITY CAT, COUNTRY CAT

City cat. Windowpane.
Cozy. Warm. Watches rain.

Country cat. Wild and free.
Stalks a mouse. Climbs a tree.

City cat. Sleek but stout.
He meows: "Let me *out*!"

Country cat. Strong but thin.
At the door: "Let me *in*!"

City cat. Window seat.
Sees the cars fill the street.

Country cat. Door ajar.
Darts inside. But not too far!

City cat. Steps outside.
Too much noise! Better hide!

Country cat. Not much fun.
Boring rooms. Time to run.

City cat. Safe and still.

Country cat. Roams at will.

This is best. There's no doubt.
One stays in. One stays out.

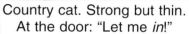
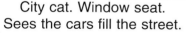

MY HELPER

He paws at the sheets,
and claws at the spread.
(My cat likes to help
when I'm making the bed.)
.

Under the blanket
he thrashes about.
Then without warning,
he scurries right out.

He plops on a pillow.
He flops on his back.
Now my pajamas
are under attack!

With such an assistant
I'll never go wrong.
His help only makes it
take three times as long.

29

WHAT IS THE WORK OF A CAT?

Sheep-herding sheepdogs will bring home the wool.
Sled-pulling sled dogs are bred just to pull.
Greyhounds win races in ten seconds flat.
But what is the work of a cat?

A guide dog will guide with a sharp pair of eyes.
A show-stopping show dog may bring home a prize.
Even my house dog can fetch me my hat.
But what is the work of a cat?

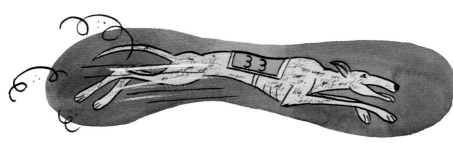

She sits on my lap while I'm brushing her fur.
She snuggles in deeper. She's starting to purr.
She makes me feel happy. Well, how about that!
That is the work of a cat!

TANDY IS TWENTY

Tandy is twenty years old today.
Her shiny black coat is speckled with gray.
She no longer scampers with kittenish glee.
She's not up for leaping, or climbing a tree.

I was just a young boy the day she was born.
The toys I gave her are tattered and torn.
Though games we played have come to an end,
she's still my companion, and I'm still her friend.

Tandy is twenty years old today.
Her shiny black coat is speckled with gray.
But stroking her neck still brings back the joy—
when she was a kitten and I was a boy.

siamese

persian

devon rex

turkish angora

himalayan

american shorthair

japanese bob

sphynx

scottish fold

american curl

ragdoll

manx

siamese · persian · devon rex · turkish angora

himalayan · american shorthair · japanese bob · sphynx

scottish fold · american curl · ragdoll · manx